Timeless Authentic Recipe from the

Indonesian Home Cooking

MINA CHEN

About Author

Mina Chen grew up in a close-knit Asian family where the kitchen was always alive with the sounds of sizzling woks, bubbling broths, and the chatter of loved ones gathered around the table. From an early age, she found herself drawn to the kitchen, learning by watching her parents and grandparents prepare cherished family recipes that had been passed down through generations. In her family, food wasn't just a part of life—it was life. Every dish told a story, held a memory, and carried with it a deep sense of heritage.

Mina's love for cooking grew alongside her curiosity about the diverse flavors and techniques found across the many regions of Asia. Over the years, she immersed herself in exploring a wide range of cuisines around Asia. Through her travels, research, and hands-on cooking experiences, she developed a deep appreciation for the cultural richness that Asian food represents.

In this cookbook, Mina brings together a curated collection of her favorite traditional and modern recipes that reflect both her heritage and her personal journey as a home cook. Each recipe is crafted with care, offering clear instructions, practical tips, and ingredients that are accessible to home kitchens around the world. Whether you're a seasoned cook or just starting out, Mina hopes her cookbook will inspire you to explore the vibrant world of Asian cuisine and create lasting memories through food—just as she has throughout her life.

History of Indonesian Food

Indonesian food is a vibrant tapestry of flavors shaped by centuries of cultural exchange, trade, and local tradition. As an archipelago of over 17,000 islands, Indonesia's cuisine reflects diverse ethnic groups, regional ingredients, and historical influences. Spices like nutmeg, cloves, and pepper drew traders from India, China, the Middle East, and later Europe, leaving lasting culinary marks. Indian influence brought rich curries and the use of spices such as turmeric and coriander, while Chinese immigrants introduced stir-frying and noodles. Arab traders contributed to the popularity of goat, lamb, and dishes like sate and nasi kebuli.

During the Dutch colonial period, European techniques and ingredients merged with local traditions, leading to fusion dishes such as rijsttafel, a grand display of multiple small plates. Indonesia's Islamic heritage influenced halal cooking practices, while Bali, predominantly Hindu, developed its own pork-based dishes. Indonesian cuisine thrives on the balance of sweet, salty, spicy, and sour, as seen in iconic foods like rendang, nasi goreng, gado-gado, and soto.

Staple ingredients such as rice, coconut, chili, palm sugar, and fermented condiments like terasi and tempeh define the national flavor. Each region boasts its own specialties—West Sumatra's fiery Padang food, Java's sweeter style, and Sulawesi's seafood-rich fare. Today, Indonesian food continues to evolve, gaining global recognition for its bold tastes and cultural richness, while remaining deeply rooted in its traditional and regional heritage.

Table of Content

About Author	3
History of Indonesian Food	4
Tahu Gejrot	9
Tahu Bakso	11
Tempe Mendoan	13
Perkedel	15
Gulai Ayam	17
Ayam Woku	19
Ayam Betutu	21
Opor Ayam	23
Ayam Bakar Taliwang	25
Ayam Goreng Lengkuas	27
Beef Rendang	29
Empal Gepuk	31
Ikan Bakar	33
Ikan Goreng	35
Soto Ayam	37
Soto Betawi	39
Bakso Kuah	41

Table of Content

About Author	3
History of Indonesian Food	4
Tahu Gejrot	9
Tahu Bakso	11
Tempe Mendoan	13
Perkedel	15
Gulai Ayam	17
Ayam Woku	19
Ayam Betutu	21
Opor Ayam	23
Ayam Bakar Taliwang	25
Ayam Goreng Lengkuas	27
Beef Rendang	29
Empal Gepuk	31
Ikan Bakar	33
Ikan Goreng	35
Soto Ayam	37
Soto Betawi	39
Bakso Kuah	41

Table of Content

Sop Buntut	43
Sop Konro	45
Rawon	47
Tongseng	49
Sate Maranggi	51
Sate Ayam	53
Sate Lilit	55
Sambal Goreng Ati	57
Telur Balado	59
Capcay	61
Gulai Nangka	63
Plecing Kangkung	65
Gado Gado	67
Terong Balado	69
Nasi Goreng	71
Mie Goreng	73
Martabak Manis	75
Es Cendol	77

Tahu Gejrot

Prep Time
20 minutes

Cooking Time
10 minutes

Serving Size
4 servings

Ingredients:

- 12 pieces fried tofu (firm or puff tofu), cut into bite-sized pieces
- 3 tbsp sweet soy sauce (kecap manis)
- 2 tbsp tamarind water (from 1 tbsp tamarind paste and 2 tbsp warm water, strained)
- 150 ml water
- 1 tbsp palm sugar or brown sugar, grated

Spice Paste (coarsely ground or crushed):

- 5 shallots
- 3 cloves garlic
- 4 bird's eye chilies (adjust to taste)
- 1/4 tsp salt

Instructions:

To prepare Tahu Gejrot, start by making the sauce. In a saucepan, combine the sweet soy sauce, tamarind water, palm sugar, and 150 ml of water. Bring the mixture to a simmer over medium heat and cook until the sugar is dissolved and the flavors blend, about 5-7 minutes. Remove from heat and set aside to cool slightly.

Meanwhile, prepare the spice paste. Using a mortar and pestle or food processor, coarsely crush the shallots, garlic, chilies, and salt until just broken down but still chunky. This rough texture gives the dish its signature bite. If your tofu is not pre-fried, deep-fry or pan-fry tofu pieces until golden and puffy, then drain on paper towels.

Place the fried tofu pieces in a serving bowl or individual small dishes. Spoon the spice paste over the tofu, then pour the slightly cooled sauce over everything. Let the tofu sit for a few minutes to soak in the sauce. Tahu Gejrot is best served at room temperature as a street-style snack or appetizer with a bold, sweet, spicy, and tangy punch in every bite.

Enjoy this flavorful Indonesian street food as a light snack or appetizer any time of day!

Tahu Bakso

Prep Time
30 minutes

Cooking Time
20 minutes

Serving Size
4 servings

Ingredients:

- 10 pieces fried tofu (firm tofu or tofu puffs), halved diagonally and hollowed slightly
- 250g ground chicken or beef
- 2 cloves garlic, minced
- 2 shallots, minced
- 1 egg
- 2 tbsp tapioca flour or cornstarch
- 1/2 tsp ground white pepper
- 1/2 tsp salt
- 1/2 tsp sugar
- 1 stalk green onion, finely sliced
- Cooking oil, for frying (optional)

For serving (optional):

- Chili sauce or sweet soy sauce
- Fresh green chilies

Instructions:

To make Tahu Bakso, start by preparing the filling. In a mixing bowl, combine the ground chicken or beef with minced garlic, shallots, egg, tapioca flour, white pepper, salt, sugar, and chopped green onion. Mix everything thoroughly until well combined and slightly sticky. This texture will help the filling stay in place when stuffed into the tofu.

Take each piece of tofu and gently open the cut edge to create a pocket. Spoon the meat mixture into the hollowed center, pressing gently to fill and smooth the surface. Repeat this process until all tofu pieces are stuffed.

You can now choose to steam or fry the tofu. To steam, arrange the stuffed tofu pieces in a steamer basket lined with parchment paper or lightly oiled, and steam over medium heat for 15–20 minutes until the filling is cooked through. If you prefer a crispy texture, you can shallow-fry the steamed tofu in a bit of oil until the surface is golden brown.

Tahu Bakso is commonly served warm with chili sauce, sweet soy sauce, or fresh green chilies on the side for a spicy kick. This savory snack is popular as street food or a side dish in Indonesia.

Enjoy this delicious combination of tofu and savory filling—perfect as a snack or light meal!

Tempe Mendoan

Prep Time
10 minutes

Cooking Time
10 minutes

Serving Size
4 servings

Ingredients:

- 200g tempeh, thinly sliced (about 10–12 pieces)
- 100g all-purpose flour
- 25g rice flour (optional, for extra crispiness)
- 2 garlic cloves, finely minced or grated
- 1/2 tsp ground coriander
- 1/2 tsp turmeric powder
- 1/2 tsp salt
- 1/4 tsp white pepper
- 150 ml water (adjust as needed for thin batter)
- 2 green onions, finely sliced
- Cooking oil, for frying

For serving (optional):
- Whole green chilies
- Sweet soy sauce (kecap manis)

Instructions:

To prepare Tempe Mendoan, begin by making the batter. In a mixing bowl, combine the all-purpose flour, rice flour, garlic, ground coriander, turmeric powder, salt, and white pepper. Gradually add water while stirring until a smooth, slightly thin batter forms. Add the sliced green onions and mix well.

Slice the tempeh into thin, wide pieces—approximately 2–3 mm thick. If you're using a block of tempeh, slice it lengthwise to maintain a larger surface area, as is traditional for mendoan.

Heat enough oil in a pan over medium heat for shallow frying. Once the oil is hot, dip each slice of tempeh into the batter, making sure it's well coated, and carefully place it in the oil. Fry just until the batter sets and the outside is lightly golden but still soft—this is what gives Tempe Mendoan its signature tender texture. Do not over-fry.

Drain the tempeh on paper towels and serve hot with whole green chilies or a small dish of sweet soy sauce for dipping.

Enjoy this deliciously savory and lightly crispy Indonesian snack, perfect for sharing with friends or as an appetizer!

Perkedel

Prep Time
25 minutes

Cooking Time
20 minutes

Serving Size
4 servings

Ingredients:

- 500g potatoes, peeled and cut into chunks
- 150g ground beef or corned beef (optional)
- 2 cloves garlic, minced
- 2 shallots, minced
- 1 egg
- 1/4 tsp ground nutmeg
- 1/2 tsp salt
- 1/4 tsp white pepper
- 1 stalk green onion, finely chopped
- Cooking oil, for frying
- 1 egg, beaten (for coating before frying)

Instructions:

Start by preparing the potatoes. Boil or deep-fry the potato chunks until soft, then drain and mash them in a large bowl until smooth. Set aside to cool slightly. If using ground beef, sauté it in a pan over medium heat with a pinch of salt and pepper until cooked through. Allow to cool before mixing into the potatoes.

To the mashed potatoes, add the cooked ground beef (or corned beef), minced garlic and shallots, egg, ground nutmeg, salt, white pepper, and chopped green onion. Mix everything thoroughly until the mixture holds together. If it feels too soft, you can chill it for a few minutes or add a spoonful of breadcrumbs or flour to firm it up.

Shape the mixture into small, flat patties, about 2 inches wide.

Heat enough oil in a frying pan over medium heat. Dip each patty gently into the beaten egg to coat the surface. Fry the patties in batches until golden brown on both sides, about 2–3 minutes per side. Avoid overcrowding the pan. Once cooked, remove and drain on paper towels.

Serve Perkedel warm as a side dish or a snack—perfect with rice, soup, or simply on its own. Enjoy this comforting Indonesian favorite!

Gulai Ayam

Prep Time
20 minutes

Cooking Time
40 minutes

Serving Size
4 servings

Ingredients:

- 1 whole chicken (about 1 kg), cut into 8-10 pieces
- 400 ml coconut milk
- 300 ml water
- 2 bay leaves (daun salam)
- 2 kaffir lime leaves
- 1 lemongrass stalk, bruised
- 2 cm galangal, bruised
- 2 tbsp cooking oil

Spice Paste (blended):

- 6 shallots
- 4 cloves garlic
- 3 candlenuts (or substitute with 2 tbsp cashews)
- 2 cm ginger
- 2 cm turmeric (or 1 tsp turmeric powder)
- 1 tsp coriander seeds or ground coriander
- 1/2 tsp cumin seeds or ground cumin
- 1-2 red chilies (adjust to taste)
- Salt and sugar to taste

Instructions:

Begin by preparing the spice paste. Blend the shallots, garlic, candlenuts, ginger, turmeric, coriander, cumin, and red chilies with a little water until smooth. Heat the cooking oil in a wok or pot over medium heat, then sauté the spice paste until fragrant and slightly thickened, about 5-7 minutes. Add the bay leaves, kaffir lime leaves, lemongrass, and galangal, stirring for another minute to release their aroma.

Add the chicken pieces to the pot and stir to coat them well with the spice mixture. Cook for a few minutes until the chicken starts to change color. Pour in the water and bring it to a boil, then reduce the heat and simmer for about 15 minutes until the chicken is half-cooked.

Add the coconut milk, stir well, and continue simmering over low heat for another 20-25 minutes until the chicken is tender and the curry is rich and flavorful. Stir occasionally to prevent the coconut milk from curdling. Adjust the taste with salt and a bit of sugar to balance the flavors.

Serve Gulai Ayam hot with steamed rice. Enjoy this comforting and aromatic Indonesian curry full of rich spices and creamy coconut goodness!

Ayam Woku

Prep Time
20 minutes

Cooking Time
30 minutes

Serving Size
4 servings

Ingredients:

- 1 whole chicken (about 1 kg), cut into 8-10 pieces
- 3 tbsp cooking oil
- 300 ml water
- Salt and sugar to taste

Spice Paste (blended):

- 6 shallots
- 4 garlic cloves
- 5 red chilies (adjust to taste)
- 3 candlenuts (or 2 tbsp cashews)
- 2 cm ginger
- 2 cm turmeric (or 1 tsp turmeric powder)
- 1 tomato

Aromatics:

- 2 lemongrass stalks, bruised
- 3 kaffir lime leaves
- 2 bay leaves (daun salam)
- 2 pandan leaves, knotted (optional)
- 2 cm galangal, bruised
- 4 spring onions, sliced
- 2 handfuls fresh basil leaves (Indonesian kemangi preferred)

Instructions:

Begin by preparing the spice paste. Blend shallots, garlic, red chilies, candlenuts, ginger, turmeric, and tomato into a smooth paste. Heat oil in a wok or large pan over medium heat and sauté the spice paste until fragrant and the oil separates slightly, about 5-7 minutes.

Add the bruised lemongrass, kaffir lime leaves, bay leaves, galangal, and pandan leaves. Stir well to release the aroma. Then, add the chicken pieces and cook until the surface turns white and the meat is coated with the spices, about 5 minutes.

Pour in the water, bring to a boil, then lower the heat and simmer for 20-25 minutes, or until the chicken is cooked through and tender. Add salt and sugar to balance the flavor as needed.

In the last few minutes of cooking, add the sliced spring onions and fresh basil leaves. Stir gently and simmer just until the basil wilts and releases its fragrance.

Serve Ayam Woku hot with steamed rice. Enjoy this bold and aromatic dish bursting with the flavors of North Sulawesi!

Ayam Betutu

Prep Time
30 minutes

Cooking Time
2 hours

Serving Size
4 servings

Ingredients:

- 1 whole chicken (about 1.2–1.5 kg), cleaned
- 3 tbsp cooking oil
- Banana leaves or foil (for wrapping)
- Salt and sugar to taste

Spice Paste (blended):

- 10 shallots
- 6 garlic cloves
- 5 red chilies (adjust to taste)
- 5 candlenuts (or 4 tbsp cashews)
- 3 cm turmeric (or 1½ tsp turmeric powder)
- 3 cm ginger
- 3 cm galangal
- 1 tsp coriander seeds
- 1/2 tsp black peppercorns
- 1 tsp shrimp paste (terasi), toasted
- Juice of 1 lime

Aromatics for stuffing and flavoring:

- 2 stalks lemongrass, bruised and cut into pieces
- 5 kaffir lime leaves, torn
- 2 bay leaves (daun salam)
- 1 tsp tamarind paste (optional)

Instructions:

Start by blending all the spice paste ingredients until smooth, adding a little oil or water to help the process if necessary. Heat cooking oil in a large pan over medium heat and sauté the spice paste until fragrant and the oil begins to separate, about 7–10 minutes. Add the tamarind paste, if using, and stir well.

Clean the whole chicken and pat it dry. Rub the chicken inside and out generously with salt, and then with the cooked spice paste, making sure it is evenly coated. Use a portion of the paste, along with the lemongrass, kaffir lime leaves, and bay leaves, to stuff the chicken cavity. Secure the opening with kitchen twine or skewers.

Wrap the entire chicken tightly in banana leaves or aluminum foil to seal in the flavors. Place the wrapped chicken in a steamer or in a roasting dish with a lid. If steaming, cook over medium heat for about 1.5 to 2 hours until the chicken is tender and infused with spices. If baking, place in a preheated oven at 180°C (350°F) and roast for the same amount of time.

Once cooked, carefully unwrap the chicken and let it rest for a few minutes before serving. You can serve it whole at the table, or cut into portions.

Enjoy Ayam Betutu with warm rice and sambal matah for an authentic Balinese feast!

Opor Ayam

Prep Time
20 minutes

Cooking Time
40 minutes

Serving Size
4 servings

Ingredients:

- 1 whole chicken (about 1–1.2 kg), cut into 8–10 pieces
- 400 ml thick coconut milk
- 300 ml water
- 3 tbsp cooking oil
- 2 bay leaves (daun salam)
- 2 kaffir lime leaves
- 1 lemongrass stalk, bruised
- 2 cm galangal, bruised
- Salt and sugar to taste

Spice Paste (blended):

- 6 shallots
- 4 garlic cloves
- 3 candlenuts (or 2 tbsp cashews)
- 2 cm ginger
- 2 cm turmeric (or 1 tsp turmeric powder)
- 1 tsp ground coriander
- 1/2 tsp white pepper

Instructions:

Begin by blending the spice paste ingredients until smooth. Heat the cooking oil in a wok or pot over medium heat, then sauté the spice paste until fragrant and slightly darkened, about 5–7 minutes. Add the bay leaves, kaffir lime leaves, lemongrass, and galangal, stirring to release their aroma.

Add the chicken pieces and stir until they are well-coated with the spices and start to change color. Pour in the water and bring it to a boil. Reduce the heat and simmer for about 15–20 minutes, or until the chicken is half-cooked and has absorbed the flavors.

Next, pour in the coconut milk, stir gently, and continue simmering over low heat for another 20 minutes until the chicken is fully cooked and the sauce is rich and slightly thickened. Stir occasionally to prevent the coconut milk from curdling. Adjust salt and sugar to taste.

Serve Opor Ayam warm with steamed rice or ketupat. Enjoy this creamy and comforting Indonesian classic!

Ayam Bakar Taliwang

Prep Time
25 minutes

Cooking Time
45 minutes

Serving Size
4 servings

Ingredients:

- 1 whole free-range chicken (about 1–1.2 kg), butterflied or halved
- 2 tbsp cooking oil
- 2 tbsp sweet soy sauce (kecap manis)
- Juice of 1 lime
- Salt to taste

Spice Paste (blended):

- 8 shallots
- 5 garlic cloves
- 10 red chilies (adjust to taste)
- 3 bird's eye chilies (optional, for extra heat)
- 3 candlenuts (or 2 tbsp cashews)
- 2 cm turmeric (or 1 tsp turmeric powder)
- 2 cm ginger
- 1 tomato
- 1 tsp toasted shrimp paste (terasi)
- 1 tsp palm sugar or brown sugar

Instructions:

Start by cleaning the chicken and splitting it open (butterfly style) so it can lay flat for grilling. Pat it dry, rub with lime juice and a bit of salt, and set aside to marinate briefly while preparing the spices.

Blend all spice paste ingredients into a smooth mixture. In a pan, heat cooking oil over medium heat and sauté the spice paste until fragrant and slightly caramelized, about 7–10 minutes. Stir in the sweet soy sauce and a bit of water to create a thick basting sauce.

Coat the chicken thoroughly with the cooked spice mixture, making sure to get the paste under the skin and into all crevices. Let it marinate for at least 30 minutes for deeper flavor (optional but recommended).

Grill the chicken over charcoal or a grill pan on medium heat, basting frequently with the remaining sauce. Cook each side for about 15–20 minutes, turning occasionally, until the chicken is cooked through and slightly charred on the outside. You can also bake the chicken at 180°C (350°F) for 30 minutes, then finish by grilling or broiling for a smoky finish.

Serve Ayam Bakar Taliwang hot with warm rice, fresh vegetables, and sambal. Enjoy this fiery and flavorful specialty from Lombok!

Ayam Goreng Lengkuas

Prep Time
20 minutes

Cooking Time
40 minutes

Serving Size
4 servings

Ingredients:

- 1 whole chicken (about 1–1.2 kg), cut into 8–10 pieces
- 200 grams fresh galangal, peeled and grated
- 4 kaffir lime leaves
- 2 bay leaves (daun salam)
- 1 stalk lemongrass, bruised
- 500 ml water (or enough to simmer chicken)
- Salt and sugar to taste
- Cooking oil for frying

Spice Paste (blended):

- 6 shallots
- 4 garlic cloves
- 3 candlenuts (or 2 tbsp cashews)
- 2 cm turmeric (or 1 tsp turmeric powder)
- 1 tsp coriander seeds
- 1/2 tsp white pepper

Instructions:

Begin by blending the spice paste ingredients until smooth. Heat a large pot or wok over medium heat and add a little oil. Sauté the spice paste until fragrant, then add the grated galangal, kaffir lime leaves, bay leaves, and lemongrass. Stir well and cook for a few minutes until aromatic.

Add the chicken pieces and stir until coated with the spices. Pour in the water and season with salt and sugar to taste. Simmer over medium heat for about 25–30 minutes until the chicken is cooked through and the liquid is mostly absorbed, leaving behind a thick layer of spices. Stir occasionally to prevent sticking.

Once the chicken is tender and the spices have reduced, remove the chicken from the pot. Set aside the remaining spice mixture (especially the galangal) to use as a crispy topping later.

Heat enough oil in a deep pan for frying. Fry the chicken pieces over medium heat until golden brown and crispy on the outside. Then, fry the remaining spice residue (grated galangal and aromatics) until crisp and golden—this will become the flavorful topping.

Drain everything on paper towels.

Serve Ayam Goreng Lengkuas hot with steamed rice and a generous sprinkle of the crispy fried galangal on top. Enjoy this fragrant Indonesian favorite!

Beef Rendang

Prep Time
30 minutes

Cooking Time
2.5 hours

Serving Size
4 servings

Ingredients:

- 600g beef chuck or brisket, cut into 2-inch cubes
- 400ml coconut milk (from 1 whole mature coconut or canned)
- 2 stalks lemongrass, bruised
- 5 kaffir lime leaves, torn
- 2 Indonesian bay leaves (daun salam) or substitute with regular bay leaves
- 1 turmeric leaf (optional), knotted
- 1 tsp salt
- 1 tsp sugar
- 1 tbsp tamarind paste

Spice Paste (blend together):

- 6 shallots
- 4 cloves garlic
- 5-6 dried red chilies (soaked in hot water until soft) or 3 fresh red chilies
- 2 cm piece galangal
- 2 cm piece ginger
- 2 cm piece turmeric (or 1 tsp ground turmeric)
- 1 tsp coriander seeds
- 1/2 tsp cumin seeds
- 1/2 tsp ground nutmeg

Instructions:

To make beef rendang, start by preparing the spice paste. Blend all the spice paste ingredients using a food processor or blender until smooth, adding a little water if needed. Set aside.

In a large wok or heavy-bottomed pot, heat a small amount of oil over medium heat and sauté the spice paste until fragrant and slightly darkened, about 5-7 minutes. Add the bruised lemongrass, kaffir lime leaves, bay leaves, and turmeric leaf if using. Stir everything well to combine and release the aromatic oils.

Next, add the beef chunks to the pot and cook until the meat is coated and sealed by the spices, about 5-10 minutes. Pour in the coconut milk and stir in the salt, sugar, and tamarind paste. Bring the mixture to a gentle boil, then reduce the heat to low and simmer uncovered. Stir occasionally to prevent sticking and allow the liquid to slowly reduce. This slow-cooking process will take around 2 to 2.5 hours.

As the liquid reduces, the color will deepen and the oil from the coconut milk will begin to separate. Continue stirring more frequently during the last 30 minutes to avoid burning. Cook until the rendang turns dark brown, the sauce thickens, and clings to the beef. The beef should be tender and flavorful, coated in the rich, spiced gravy. Serve hot with steamed. Enjoy!

Empal Gepuk

Prep Time
30 minutes

Cooking Time
1.5 hours

Serving Size
4 servings

Ingredients:

- 500 grams beef (preferably shank or brisket), cut into thick slices
- 500 ml water (for boiling)
- 2 bay leaves (daun salam)
- 1 stalk lemongrass, bruised
- 1 kaffir lime leaf
- 2 tbsp grated coconut (optional, for richer flavor)
- 2 tbsp palm sugar or brown sugar
- Salt to taste
- Oil for frying

Spice Paste (blended):
- 6 shallots
- 4 garlic cloves
- 3 candlenuts (or 2 tbsp cashews)
- 2 cm galangal
- 2 cm ginger
- 1 tsp ground coriander
- 1/2 tsp white pepper

Instructions:

Start by pounding the beef slices slightly with a meat mallet to tenderize and allow the flavors to penetrate better. Set aside.

Blend all the spice paste ingredients until smooth. Heat a little oil in a pan and sauté the spice paste with bay leaves, lemongrass, and kaffir lime leaf until fragrant and the oil begins to separate, about 5–7 minutes. Add the beef slices and stir until they are well-coated with the spices.

Pour in the water and bring it to a boil. Add the grated coconut if using, palm sugar, and salt to taste. Reduce the heat and simmer uncovered for about 1 hour, or until the beef is tender and the liquid has mostly evaporated, leaving a thick coating of spices on the meat. Stir occasionally to prevent burning.

Once the beef is tender and coated in the reduced spice mixture, remove from heat and gently pound each piece with a pestle or flat object until slightly shredded but still intact—this is the signature "geprek" or smashing step of Empal Gepuk.

Heat enough oil in a frying pan and shallow-fry the beef over medium heat until the outside is brown and slightly crispy, just a few minutes per side. Be careful not to over-fry as the beef is already cooked.

Serve Empal Gepuk warm with steamed rice, sambal, and fresh vegetables or lalapan. Enjoy the sweet, savory, and slightly crispy Sundanese delicacy!

Ikan Bakar

Prep Time
25 minnutes

Cooking Time
30 minutes

Serving Size
4 servings

Ingredients:

- 2 medium-sized tilapia, cleaned and scored
- Juice of 1 lime
- Salt to taste
- 2 tbsp sweet soy sauce (kecap manis)
- 2 tbsp cooking oil

Spice Paste (blended):

- 6 shallots
- 4 garlic cloves
- 5 red chilies (adjust to taste)
- 3 candlenuts (or 2 tbsp cashews)
- 2 cm turmeric (or 1 tsp turmeric powder)
- 2 cm galangal
- 1 stalk lemongrass (white part only)
- 1 tsp coriander seeds
- 1 tsp palm sugar or brown sugar
- 1 tsp salt

Instructions:

Begin by cleaning the tilapia thoroughly. Score the surface on both sides to allow the marinade to penetrate deeply. Rub the fish with lime juice and a little salt, then let it sit for about 10 minutes to remove any fishy odor.

While the fish is marinating, blend all the spice paste ingredients until smooth. Heat a little oil in a pan and sauté the spice paste until fragrant and slightly caramelized. Turn off the heat and mix in the sweet soy sauce. Let the marinade cool slightly.

Coat the tilapia evenly with the cooked spice paste, making sure it gets into the scored areas and the cavity of the fish. Let it marinate for at least 15 minutes (or up to 1 hour for stronger flavor).

Preheat your grill or grill pan over medium heat. Brush the grill with oil to prevent sticking. Grill the fish for about 7–10 minutes on each side, or until the skin is charred and the fish is cooked through. While grilling, occasionally brush with leftover marinade or a little oil to keep the fish moist and flavorful.

Serve Ikan Bakar hot with steamed rice, sambal terasi, and fresh vegetables or lalapan. Enjoy this aromatic and smoky Indonesian grilled fish!

Ikan Goreng

Prep Time
25 minutes

Cooking Time
20 minutes

Serving Size
4 servings

Ingredients:

- 2 medium-sized tilapia, cleaned and scored
- Juice of 1 lime
- 1 tsp salt
- 1/2 tsp turmeric powder
- 1/2 tsp coriander powder
- 2 cloves garlic, finely grated
- Oil for deep frying

Instructions:

Clean the tilapia thoroughly and score the surface on both sides to help the seasoning penetrate. Rub the fish with lime juice and a pinch of salt, then let it sit for 10 minutes to reduce any fishy odor. Rinse briefly and pat dry with paper towels.

In a small bowl, mix turmeric powder, coriander powder, grated garlic, and salt with a splash of water to make a thick paste. Rub this seasoning mixture all over the fish, making sure to get it into the scored areas and inside the cavity. Let the fish marinate for about 10–15 minutes.

Heat enough oil in a deep frying pan over medium heat. Once the oil is hot, carefully lower the fish into the pan, one at a time if necessary, to avoid overcrowding. Fry each side for about 6–8 minutes or until golden brown and crispy. Flip the fish carefully to avoid breaking the skin.

Once done, remove the fish from the oil and drain on paper towels to remove excess oil.

Serve Ikan Goreng hot with steamed rice, sambal terasi, and fresh vegetables (lalapan) for a simple yet satisfying Indonesian meal. Enjoy this crispy and flavorful fried fish!

Soto Ayam

Prep Time
20 minutes

Cooking Time
45 minutes

Serving Size
4 servings

Ingredients:

- 500 grams bone-in chicken
- 1.5 liters water
- 2 bay leaves
- 2 kaffir lime leaves
- 1 stalk lemongrass, bruised
- 1 thumb-sized piece of galangal, bruised
- Salt and pepper to taste
- 2 tbsp oil (for sautéing)

Spice Paste (blended):
- 6 shallots
- 4 garlic cloves
- 3 candlenuts (or 2 tbsp cashews)
- 2 cm turmeric (or 1 tsp turmeric powder)
- 2 cm ginger
- 1 tsp coriander powder
- 1/2 tsp white pepper

For serving:
- Cooked rice or vermicelli noodles
- Hard-boiled eggs, halved
- Bean sprouts, blanched
- Shredded cabbage
- Fried shallots
- Lime wedges
- Sambal
- Fresh celery leaves or spring onions, chopped

Instructions:

Start by boiling the chicken in 1.5 liters of water with bay leaves, kaffir lime leaves, lemongrass, and galangal. Let it simmer over medium heat until the chicken is fully cooked, about 30 minutes. Remove the chicken from the broth and set it aside to cool slightly, then shred the meat into thin pieces. Strain the broth if necessary and keep it warm.

While the chicken is cooking, prepare the spice paste by blending all the paste ingredients until smooth. Heat the oil in a pan and sauté the spice paste over medium heat until fragrant and the oil starts to separate, about 5–7 minutes.

Add the cooked spice paste to the chicken broth and stir well. Simmer for another 10–15 minutes to allow the flavors to infuse. Season with salt and pepper to taste.

To serve, place a portion of rice or vermicelli noodles in a bowl. Top with shredded chicken, bean sprouts, cabbage, and a halved boiled egg. Ladle the hot broth over the toppings. Garnish with fried shallots, chopped celery or spring onions, and serve with lime wedges and sambal on the side.

Enjoy Soto Ayam, a comforting and aromatic Indonesian chicken soup perfect for any time of day!

Soto Betawi

Prep Time
25 minutes

Cooking Time
1.5 hours

Serving Size
4 servings

Ingredients:

- 500 grams beef brisket or shank, cut into chunks
- 1 liter water
- 400 ml coconut milk
- 200 ml fresh milk or evaporated milk
- 2 bay leaves
- 2 kaffir lime leaves
- 1 stalk lemongrass, bruised
- 2 cm galangal, bruised
- Salt and sugar to taste
- 2 tbsp cooking oil

Spice Paste (blended):
- 6 shallots
- 4 garlic cloves
- 3 candlenuts
- 1 tsp coriander seeds
- 1/2 tsp cumin seeds
- 1/2 tsp white pepper
- 2 cm ginger
- 2 cm turmeric (or 1 tsp turmeric powder)

For Serving:
- Fried potato cubes
- Tomato wedges
- Sliced celery and green onion
- Fried shallots
- Lime wedges
- Emping (melinjo crackers)
- Sambal

Instructions:

Begin by boiling the beef chunks in 1 liter of water over medium heat until tender, about 1 hour. Skim off any foam that rises to the surface. Once the beef is tender, remove and set it aside. Strain the broth to remove impurities and set the broth aside as well.

In the meantime, prepare the spice paste by blending the shallots, garlic, candlenuts, coriander, cumin, pepper, ginger, and turmeric until smooth. Heat oil in a pan and sauté the spice paste along with bay leaves, kaffir lime leaves, lemongrass, and galangal until aromatic and the oil begins to separate.

Return the cooked beef to the pot with the strained broth. Add the sautéed spice mixture, then pour in the coconut milk and fresh milk. Simmer over low heat for another 30 minutes, stirring occasionally to prevent curdling. Season with salt and sugar to taste.

To serve, place beef chunks and fried potato cubes in a bowl. Pour the hot broth over and top with tomato wedges, sliced celery and green onion, and fried shallots. Serve with lime wedges, emping crackers, and sambal on the side.

Enjoy Soto Betawi, the rich and creamy beef soup from Jakarta that's bursting with traditional Indonesian flavors!

Bakso Kuah

Prep Time
30 minutes

Cooking Time
40 minutes

Serving Size
4 servings

Ingredients:

For the meatballs (bakso):
- 300 grams ground beef
- 100 grams tapioca flour
- 2 garlic cloves, minced
- 1 egg white
- 1 tsp salt
- 1/2 tsp pepper
- 1/2 tsp sugar
- Ice water as needed

For the broth:
- 1.5 liters water
- 3 garlic cloves, smashed and sautéed until golden
- 1 stalk celery, tied
- 1 spring onion, tied
- 1 beef bouillon cube (optional)
- Salt and pepper to taste

For serving:
- Cooked yellow noodles or vermicelli
- Bok choy or mustard greens, blanched
- Fried shallots
- Sliced celery or spring onion
- Sambal and lime wedges
- Sweet soy sauce

Instructions:

Start by making the meatballs. In a food processor, blend the ground beef with garlic, salt, pepper, sugar, and egg white until smooth. Gradually add tapioca flour and a little ice water to help the mixture blend. The texture should be thick and slightly sticky. Wet your hands and shape the mixture into small balls, about the size of a ping pong ball.

Bring a large pot of water to a boil, then reduce to a simmer. Drop the meatballs into the water; they will sink at first and float when cooked. Once all meatballs are cooked and floating, remove them and set aside.

To make the broth, boil 1.5 liters of water in a separate pot. Add the sautéed garlic, tied celery and spring onion, and beef bouillon cube if using. Season with salt and pepper to taste. Let the broth simmer for 20–30 minutes for maximum flavor. Remove the celery and spring onion.

Add the cooked meatballs into the hot broth and simmer for a few more minutes to allow flavors to meld.

To serve, place cooked noodles and blanched greens in a bowl, add the hot meatballs and broth, and garnish with fried shallots, sliced celery or spring onion, and a squeeze of lime. Offer sambal and sweet soy sauce on the side to adjust to taste.

Enjoy this comforting bowl of Bakso Kuah—Indonesia's beloved street food classic!

Sop Buntut

Prep Time
30 minutes

Cooking Time
2 hours

Serving Size
4 servings

Ingredients:

- 1 kg oxtail, cut into pieces
- 2 liters water
- 2 carrots, peeled and cut into chunks
- 2 potatoes, peeled and cut into chunks
- 2 tomatoes, quartered
- 1 stalk celery, tied
- 1 leek or green onion, tied
- 1 cinnamon stick
- 3 cloves
- 1 nutmeg, cracked
- 2 tbsp cooking oil

Spice Paste (blend until smooth):
- 6 shallots
- 4 garlic cloves
- 1/2 tsp white pepper
- Salt and sugar to taste

For serving:
- Fried shallots
- Chopped celery and spring onion
- Lime wedges
- Sambal

Instructions:

Start by boiling the oxtail in a large pot of water for a few minutes until foam and impurities rise to the top. Discard the water, rinse the oxtail, and set aside. In a clean pot, bring 2 liters of fresh water to a boil. Add the cleaned oxtail.

Heat oil in a pan and sauté the blended spice paste until fragrant. Add the cinnamon stick, cloves, and nutmeg, then continue sautéing for another minute. Add the mixture to the simmering oxtail pot. Add tied celery and leek to infuse flavor into the broth and simmer over low heat for about 1.5 to 2 hours, or until the meat is tender. Skim the surface regularly to keep the broth clear.

After about 1.5 hours, when the oxtail is nearly tender, add the carrot and potato chunks. Cook until they are tender but not mushy, about 20 minutes. Add the quartered tomatoes last and simmer for another 5–10 minutes. Adjust the seasoning with salt and sugar as needed.

To serve, ladle the hot oxtail soup into bowls, making sure each serving has generous chunks of meat and vegetables. Garnish with fried shallots, chopped celery, and spring onion. Serve with lime wedges and sambal on the side.

Enjoy this hearty and aromatic Sop Buntut, a true comfort dish in Indonesian cuisine!

Sop Konro

Prep Time
30 minutes

Cooking Time
2 hours

Serving Size
4 servings

Ingredients:

- 1 kg beef ribs (short ribs or back ribs)
- 2 liters water
- 2 bay leaves
- 2 stalks lemongrass, bruised
- 3 kaffir lime leaves
- 1 thumb-length piece of galangal, bruised
- Salt and sugar to taste
- 2 tbsp tamarind water (or to taste)
- 2 tbsp cooking oil

Spice Paste (blend until smooth):

- 8 shallots
- 5 garlic cloves
- 4 candlenuts
- 1 tbsp coriander seeds, toasted
- 1/2 tsp black peppercorns
- 1/2 tsp cumin seeds, toasted
- 1/2 tsp nutmeg powder
- 1 tbsp ground turmeric

For serving (optional):

- Fried shallots
- Chopped celery or spring onion
- Lime wedges
- Rice or ketupat (rice cake)
- Sambal

Instructions:

Begin by boiling the beef ribs in a large pot of water over medium heat. Allow it to boil until the scum rises to the surface, then discard the water. Rinse the ribs and clean the pot. Refill with 2 liters of fresh water, add the ribs back in, and bring to a boil again. Reduce the heat and simmer gently for 1.5 to 2 hours, or until the meat is tender and the broth is rich. Skim off any impurities that rise to the top.

Meanwhile, heat cooking oil in a pan and sauté the blended spice paste until fragrant and the oil begins to separate, about 5–7 minutes. Add bay leaves, bruised lemongrass, kaffir lime leaves, and galangal. Continue to sauté for a few minutes to release their aroma.

Once the spice mixture is ready, add it to the simmering beef ribs. Stir well and let everything simmer together so the flavors infuse into the broth. Add tamarind water, salt, and sugar to taste. Simmer for another 15–20 minutes, adjusting seasoning as needed.

To serve, place the ribs in deep bowls and pour over the rich, spiced broth. Garnish with fried shallots and chopped celery or spring onion. Serve with rice or ketupat and sambal on the side, with lime wedges for added brightness.

Enjoy this bold and savory Sop Konro, a signature dish from South Sulawesi that's perfect for a hearty meal.

Rawon

Prep Time
30 minutes

Cooking Time
2 hours

Serving Size
4 servings

Ingredients:

- 500 g beef shank or brisket, cut into cubes
- 2 liters water
- 3 kaffir lime leaves
- 2 lemongrass stalks, bruised
- 1 bay leaf
- Salt and sugar to taste
- 3 tbsp cooking oil

Spice Paste (blend until smooth):
- 6 shallots
- 4 garlic cloves
- 2 cm fresh turmeric (or 1 tsp ground turmeric)
- 2 cm galangal
- 4 candlenuts
- 1 tsp coriander seeds, toasted
- 1/2 tsp black pepper
- 1 tsp shrimp paste (terasi), toasted
- 5–6 kluwek (pangium) nuts, flesh scooped out (or 2–3 tbsp kluwek paste)

For serving (optional):
- Steamed rice
- Bean sprouts
- Boiled salted egg
- Fried shallots
- Sliced spring onions
- Sambal
- Lime wedges
- Kerupuk (Indonesian crackers)

Instructions:

Begin by boiling the beef in 2 liters of water. Once it comes to a boil and scum rises to the surface, skim off the foam and reduce the heat to a simmer. Let the beef cook gently for about 1.5 to 2 hours or until tender, keeping the broth clear by occasionally skimming the surface.

While the beef simmers, prepare the spice paste. Blend all the spice paste ingredients into a smooth mixture. Heat the cooking oil in a pan, then sauté the spice paste over medium heat until fragrant and slightly darkened, about 5–7 minutes. Add the kaffir lime leaves, bay leaf, and lemongrass. Sauté for another minute to bring out the aroma.

Once the beef is tender, add the sautéed spice mixture to the broth. Stir well to combine. Season the soup with salt and sugar to taste. Simmer for an additional 20–30 minutes to allow the flavors to fully develop. If the broth becomes too thick, add a little hot water to adjust the consistency.

To serve, place a portion of steamed rice in each bowl. Ladle the rich black beef soup over the rice, making sure each portion has plenty of meat. Top with bean sprouts, boiled salted egg halves, fried shallots, and sliced spring onions. Serve with sambal, lime wedges, and kerupuk on the side.

Enjoy the deep, earthy, and savory flavors of Rawon – a classic East Javanese specialty!

Tongseng

Prep Time
20 minutes

Cooking Time
45 minutes

Serving Size
4 servings

Ingredients:

- 500 g beef or mutton (boneless), thinly sliced
- 2 tbsp cooking oil
- 400 ml water
- 200 ml coconut milk
- 3 kaffir lime leaves
- 1 lemongrass stalk, bruised
- 2 Indonesian bay leaves (daun salam)
- 1 medium tomato, cut into wedges
- 4 bird's eye chili (whole)
- 100 g cabbage, roughly chopped
- 2 tbsp sweet soy sauce (kecap manis)
- Salt and sugar to taste

Spice Paste (blend until smooth):

- 6 shallots
- 4 garlic cloves
- 2 candlenuts
- 1 tsp coriander seeds
- 2 cm ginger
- 2 cm galangal
- 1/2 tsp white pepper

For serving (optional):

- Steamed rice
- Fried shallots
- Pickles (acar)

Instructions:

Start by prepare the spice paste. Blend all the spice paste ingredients into a smooth mixture. Heat the cooking oil in a wok or pot over medium heat. Add the blended spice paste and sauté until fragrant, about 5 minutes. Add the kaffir lime leaves, lemongrass, and bay leaves, continuing to stir until the spices are well cooked and aromatic.

Next, add the sliced meat to the pot and stir to coat it evenly with the spices. Cook for 5-7 minutes until the meat starts to brown. Pour in the water and bring to a boil. Lower the heat and simmer for about 25-30 minutes, or until the meat becomes tender.

Once the meat is tender, pour in the coconut milk and stir gently. Add the sweet soy sauce, chopped cabbage, tomato wedges, and bird's eye chili. Simmer for another 5-10 minutes until the vegetables are tender but still slightly crisp. Season with salt and sugar to taste, adjusting the balance of savory and sweetness according to your preference.

To serve, ladle the Tongseng into bowls and garnish with fried shallots if desired. Serve hot with steamed rice and a side of acar (pickled vegetables) for a refreshing contrast.

Enjoy this comforting and flavorful Tongseng – a Central Javanese favorite with a perfect blend of spice and sweetness.

Sate Maranggi

Prep Time
2 hours

Cooking Time
20 minutes

Serving Size
4 servings

Ingredients:

For the satay:
- 500 g beef sirloin or tenderloin, cut into 2 cm cubes
- Bamboo skewers, soaked in water for 30 minutes

Marinade:
- 4 garlic cloves
- 6 shallots
- 1 tbsp coriander seeds, toasted
- 2 tbsp sweet soy sauce (kecap manis)
- 1 tbsp tamarind water
- 1 tbsp palm sugar (or brown sugar)
- 1 tsp salt
- 1/2 tsp black pepper

For sambal kecap (sweet soy dipping sauce):
- 4 tbsp sweet soy sauce (kecap manis)
- 4 shallots, thinly sliced
- 1 tomato, finely diced
- 2–3 bird's eye chilies, thinly sliced (adjust to taste)
- 1 tbsp lime juice

Instructions:

To prepare the marinade, grind the garlic, shallots, and toasted coriander seeds into a smooth paste using a mortar and pestle or food processor. Mix the spice paste with sweet soy sauce, tamarind water, palm sugar, salt, and black pepper until well combined. Place the beef cubes into a bowl and pour the marinade over them. Mix thoroughly to ensure all pieces are well coated. Cover and refrigerate for at least 2 hours, preferably overnight for deeper flavor.

Thread the marinated beef onto the soaked bamboo skewers. Preheat a charcoal grill or grill pan over medium-high heat. Grill the satay for about 2–3 minutes on each side, or until the meat is nicely charred and cooked through, basting occasionally with the leftover marinade for extra flavor.

While the satay is grilling, prepare the sambal kecap. In a small bowl, mix together sweet soy sauce, sliced shallots, diced tomato, bird's eye chilies, and lime juice. Stir well and set aside.

Once the satay is done, serve it hot with steamed rice or lontong (rice cakes), accompanied by the sambal kecap for dipping.

Enjoy the smoky-sweet and savory goodness of Sate Maranggi – a beloved Sundanese specialty perfect for grilling sessions.

Sate Ayam

Prep Time
1 hour

Cooking Time
20 minutes

Serving Size
4 servings

Ingredients:

For the chicken satay:
- 500 g boneless chicken thighs or breast, cut into 2 cm cubes
- Bamboo skewers, soaked in water for 30 minutes

Marinade:
- 3 cloves garlic
- 5 shallots
- 1 tsp coriander seeds
- 1 tsp turmeric powder
- 1 tbsp sweet soy sauce (kecap manis)
- 1 tbsp palm sugar or brown sugar
- 1 tbsp oil
- 1/2 tsp salt

For the peanut sauce:
- 150 g roasted peanuts, ground or blended
- 3 cloves garlic
- 3 bird's eye chilies (adjust to taste)
- 2 tbsp sweet soy sauce (kecap manis)
- 1 tbsp palm sugar or brown sugar
- 1/2 tsp salt
- 200 ml water
- 1 tbsp lime juice

For garnish and serving (optional):
- Fried shallots
- Lontong (rice cakes) or steamed rice
- Slices of cucumber and shallots

Instructions:

Begin by preparing the marinade. Blend or grind the garlic, shallots, and coriander seeds into a smooth paste. Mix in turmeric powder, sweet soy sauce, palm sugar, oil, and salt. Combine the marinade with the chicken pieces in a bowl, ensuring each piece is well coated. Cover and refrigerate for at least 1 hour to allow the flavors to develop.

While the chicken marinates, make the peanut sauce. Blend or grind the garlic and chilies into a paste. In a small saucepan, heat a little oil and sauté the paste until fragrant. Add the ground peanuts, sweet soy sauce, palm sugar, salt, and water. Stir and simmer over low heat until the sauce thickens, about 5–10 minutes. Add lime juice to balance the flavor, then remove from heat and set aside.

Thread the marinated chicken pieces onto the soaked skewers. Preheat a charcoal grill or grill pan over medium-high heat. Grill the satay, turning occasionally and basting with leftover marinade, until the chicken is cooked through and lightly charred, about 2–3 minutes per side.

Serve the sate ayam hot, generously drizzled with peanut sauce and topped with fried shallots if desired. Accompany with lontong or steamed rice, and fresh cucumber and shallot slices for a refreshing contrast.

Enjoy the rich, smoky flavor of Sate Ayam – a classic and beloved Indonesian street food favorite.

Sate Lilit

Prep Time
25 minutes

Cooking Time
15 minutes

Serving Size
4 servings

Ingredients:

- 400 g minced chicken, fish, or pork (traditional uses tuna or chicken)
- 8 lemongrass stalks (use the thick bottom part for skewers)
- 1/2 cup grated coconut (fresh or desiccated)
- 1 egg
- 1 tbsp vegetable oil
- 1 tsp salt
- 1/2 tsp pepper

Spice paste (Base Gede):

- 4 shallots
- 3 garlic cloves
- 2 red chilies (adjust to taste)
- 2 candlenuts
- 2 tsp turmeric powder (or 2 cm fresh turmeric)
- 1 tsp coriander seeds
- 1/2 tsp nutmeg
- 1/2 tsp ginger (or galangal)
- 1 tbsp palm sugar
- 1 tbsp lime juice
- 1 tbsp fish sauce (optional)

Instructions:

Start by preparing the spice paste. Blend or grind all the spice paste ingredients into a smooth mixture using a food processor or mortar and pestle. If needed, add a little oil or water to help the blending process. In a pan, heat a tablespoon of oil over medium heat and sauté the spice paste until fragrant and cooked through, about 5 minutes. Allow it to cool slightly.

In a large mixing bowl, combine the minced meat with the grated coconut, sautéed spice paste, egg, salt, and pepper. Mix everything thoroughly until the mixture is sticky and well combined. If the mixture feels too wet, you can add a bit more grated coconut or a spoonful of rice flour.

Trim the lemongrass stalks to about 15 cm, peeling off the outer tough layers to expose the tender inner stalk. Take a small handful of the meat mixture and mold it around the end of each lemongrass stalk, pressing it tightly to form an oval-shaped satay.

Heat a grill pan or charcoal grill over medium heat. Lightly oil the surface and grill the satay, turning occasionally, until the meat is fully cooked and slightly charred, about 10–15 minutes.

Serve the Sate Lilit hot, garnished with fresh herbs or sambal matah, and enjoy with steamed rice or nasi campur for a complete Balinese-style meal.

Enjoy the aromatic and flavorful taste of Sate Lilit – Bali's unique twist on satay, infused with lemongrass and spices.

Sambal Goreng Ati

Prep Time
20 minutes

Cooking Time
30 minutes

Serving Size
4 servings

Ingredients:

- 300 g chicken liver (ati), cleaned and cut into bite-size pieces
- 2 medium potatoes, peeled and diced
- 2 bay leaves
- 1 lemongrass stalk, bruised
- 1 kaffir lime leaf (optional)
- 200 ml coconut milk
- 1 tsp salt
- 1/2 tsp sugar
- Oil for frying and sautéing

Spice paste:
- 6 shallots
- 4 garlic cloves
- 5 red chilies (adjust to taste)
- 2 candlenuts
- 1 tsp shrimp paste (terasi), toasted

Instructions:

Begin by frying the diced potatoes in hot oil until golden and crispy. Remove and drain on paper towels. Then, in the same oil or fresh oil, fry the chicken liver pieces until browned and just cooked through. Set them aside.

Prepare the spice paste by blending or grinding the shallots, garlic, red chilies, candlenuts, and toasted shrimp paste until smooth. In a wok or large pan, heat 2 tablespoons of oil over medium heat and sauté the spice paste until fragrant and the oil separates, about 5 minutes.

Add the bay leaves, bruised lemongrass, and kaffir lime leaf, stirring to release their aroma. Then, add the fried liver and potatoes to the pan, stirring to coat them evenly with the spice mixture. Pour in the coconut milk and season with salt and sugar.

Simmer the mixture over low heat, stirring occasionally, until the sauce thickens and coats the liver and potatoes, about 10–15 minutes. Adjust seasoning to taste, then remove from heat.

Serve Sambal Goreng Ati warm with steamed rice as part of a complete Indonesian meal.

Enjoy the rich and spicy flavor of Sambal Goreng Ati – a classic dish with bold taste and hearty texture.

Telur Balado

Prep Time
15 minutes

Cooking Time
25 minutes

Serving Size
4 servings

Ingredients:

- 8 hard-boiled eggs, peeled
- 5 red chilies (or to taste)
- 3 shallots
- 2 garlic cloves
- 1 large tomato, chopped
- 1 kaffir lime leaf (optional)
- 1 tbsp lime juice or tamarind water
- 1/2 tsp sugar
- 1/2 tsp salt
- Oil for frying and sautéing

Instructions:

Start by deep-frying or pan-frying the hard-boiled eggs in hot oil until the outer surface becomes lightly golden and blistered. This helps the sambal cling better to the eggs later. Remove the eggs and set them aside.

Blend the red chilies, shallots, garlic, and tomato into a coarse paste using a blender or mortar and pestle. Heat 2 tablespoons of oil in a pan over medium heat, then sauté the chili paste until fragrant and the oil starts to separate, around 7–10 minutes. Add the kaffir lime leaf, lime juice (or tamarind water), sugar, and salt. Stir well and cook for another few minutes until the sambal thickens.

Add the fried eggs into the sambal and gently stir to coat them evenly in the spicy sauce. Simmer on low heat for another 5 minutes to let the flavors absorb.

Serve Telur Balado warm with steamed rice and enjoy the bold, spicy, and savory flavor of this beloved Indonesian dish.

Enjoy Telur Balado – a fiery favorite that's simple yet bursting with flavor!

Capcay

Prep Time
20 minutes

Cooking Time
15 minutes

Serving Size
4 servings

Ingredients:

- 2 tbsp vegetable oil
- 3 cloves garlic, minced
- 1/2 onion, thinly sliced (optional)
- 100 g boneless chicken breast, thinly sliced
- 5-6 shiitake mushrooms, sliced
- 100 g cauliflower florets
- 100 g broccoli florets
- 1 small carrot, sliced diagonally
- 100 g bok choy or napa cabbage, chopped
- 50 g shimeji mushrooms (brown and white)
- 2-3 slices red chili (for topping)
- 200 ml chicken broth or water
- 1 tbsp oyster sauce
- 1 tbsp soy sauce
- 1 tsp sesame oil
- 1 tsp cornstarch mixed with 2 tbsp water
- Salt and pepper to taste
- Sliced green onions (for garnish)

Instructions:

Heat vegetable oil in a wok over medium-high heat. Sauté the minced garlic until fragrant. Add the sliced chicken breast and stir-fry until it turns white and is nearly cooked through. Add the shiitake mushrooms, followed by the cauliflower, broccoli, and carrots. Stir-fry for a few minutes until the vegetables start to soften but are still crisp.

Add the chopped bok choy and shimeji mushrooms to the wok. Pour in the chicken broth or water and bring to a simmer. Stir in the oyster sauce, soy sauce, sesame oil, and season with salt and pepper. Let the mixture simmer for 2-3 minutes to allow the flavors to blend and the vegetables to finish cooking.

Once the vegetables are tender-crisp and the chicken is fully cooked, stir in the cornstarch slurry and cook until the sauce thickens to your desired consistency. Remove from heat and transfer to a serving dish.

Top the Capcay with sliced red chilies for a pop of heat and color, and garnish with fresh green onions. Serve hot with steamed rice. Enjoy!

Gulai Nangka

Prep Time
20 minutes

Cooking Time
40 minutes

Serving Size
4 servings

Ingredients:

- 500 g young jackfruit (nangka muda), cut into chunks
- 200 g green bean, sliced
- 400 ml coconut milk
- 500 ml water
- 2 bay leaves
- 2 kaffir lime leaves
- 1 lemongrass stalk, bruised
- 2 tbsp cooking oil
- Salt and sugar to taste

Spice paste:

- 6 shallots
- 4 garlic cloves
- 3 red chilies
- 3 candlenuts
- 2 tsp ground coriander
- 1 tsp turmeric powder
- 1 tsp ground galangal
- 1 tsp ground ginger

Instructions:

Begin by boiling the young jackfruit chunks in water for about 10–15 minutes to reduce bitterness and soften the texture slightly. Drain and set aside.

Meanwhile, prepare the spice paste by blending the shallots, garlic, chilies, candlenuts, coriander, turmeric, galangal, and ginger until smooth. In a large pot or wok, heat the cooking oil over medium heat, then sauté the spice paste until fragrant and the oil begins to separate, about 5–7 minutes. Add the bay leaves, kaffir lime leaves, and lemongrass, stirring for another minute.

Add the pre-boiled jackfruit chunks to the pan, stir well to coat them in the spices, then pour in the water and bring it to a gentle boil. Simmer for 10 minutes to allow the jackfruit to absorb the flavor. Add the sliced green bean, stir well. Pour in the coconut milk, season with salt and sugar to taste, and simmer over low heat for another 20 minutes, stirring occasionally to prevent curdling.

Once the curry has thickened and the jackfruit is tender and flavorful, remove from heat.

Serve warm with steamed rice and enjoy the rich and aromatic taste of Gulai Nangka – a beloved Indonesian comfort dish.

Plecing Kangkung

Prep Time
15 minutes

Cooking Time
10 minutes

Serving Size
4 servings

Ingredients:

- 2 bunches of kangkung (water spinach), trimmed and cleaned
- Salt for boiling water

Sambal Plecing:
- 5 red chilies (adjust to taste)
- 3 bird's eye chilies (optional, for extra heat)
- 3 shallots
- 2 garlic cloves
- 1 medium tomato, cut into chunks
- 1 tsp toasted shrimp paste (terasi), optional
- 1 tbsp lime juice
- 1 tsp salt
- 1 tsp sugar

For Serving:
- Lime wedges
- Fried or roasted peanut

Instructions:

Bring a large pot of salted water to a boil. Add the kangkung and blanch for about 1–2 minutes until the greens are wilted but still vibrant. Drain immediately and plunge into cold water to stop the cooking process and preserve the color. Drain again and set aside.

To prepare the sambal, boil the red chilies, bird's eye chilies, shallots, garlic, and tomato for about 5 minutes until slightly softened. Drain, then blend or grind the boiled ingredients with the toasted shrimp paste (if using), salt, sugar, and lime juice into a coarse sambal. Adjust the seasoning to your taste.

To serve, place the blanched kangkung on a plate and generously spoon the sambal over the top. Serve with fried peanut and lime wedges on the side.

Enjoy Plecing Kangkung as a spicy, refreshing side dish that pairs perfectly with grilled or fried Indonesian dishes.

Gado Gado

Prep Time
25 minutes

Cooking Time
15 minutes

Serving Size
4 servings

Ingredients:

Vegetables and accompaniments:

- 200 g cabbage, shredded and blanched
- 200 g bean sprouts, blanched
- 150 g green beans, cut into 5 cm lengths and blanched
- 2 medium potatoes, boiled and sliced
- 2 hard-boiled eggs, halved
- 1 cucumber, sliced
- 4 tomato cherry, halved (optional)
- 1 block of tofu, fried and cubed
- 1 block of tempeh, fried and sliced
- Lontong (rice cake), cut into cubes (optional)
- Fried shallots and krupuk (crackers) for garnish

Peanut sauce:

- 200 g roasted peanuts
- 3 garlic cloves
- 3 red chilies (adjust to taste)
- 2 tbsp palm sugar (or brown sugar)
- 1 tbsp tamarind paste
- 1 tsp salt
- 300 ml water (adjust for consistency)
- 1 tbsp sweet soy sauce (kecap manis)
- 1 tsp lime juice

Instructions:

Start by preparing all the vegetables. Blanch the cabbage, bean sprouts, and green beans separately in boiling water for 1–2 minutes each, then drain and set aside. Boil the potatoes until soft, peel if desired, then slice them. Fry the tofu and tempeh until golden brown and crispy, then set aside. Boil the eggs, peel, and cut them in half. Prepare sliced cucumber, halved tomato, and cut the rice cake if using.

To make the peanut sauce, blend the roasted peanuts, garlic, red chilies, and palm sugar into a coarse paste. In a saucepan, heat a small amount of oil and sauté the paste briefly until fragrant. Add tamarind paste, salt, and water, stirring continuously until the sauce thickens. Add sweet soy sauce and lime juice, mix well, and adjust consistency and flavor to your liking.

To serve, arrange all the vegetables, potatoes, tofu, tempeh, cucumber, and eggs on a plate. Pour the warm peanut sauce generously over the top. Garnish with fried shallots and serve with krupuk on the side.

Enjoy this colorful and nutritious Indonesian dish full of textures and bold flavors – Gado-Gado!

Terong Balado

Prep Time
15 minutes

Cooking Time
20 minutes

Serving Size
4 servings

Ingredients:

- 2 large eggplants (terong), cut lengthwise into wedges
- 1/2 tsp salt
- Oil for frying

Balado sambal:

- 5 red chilies (adjust to taste)
- 3 bird's eye chilies (optional, for extra heat)
- 5 shallots
- 3 garlic cloves
- 2 medium tomatoes, chopped
- 1 tsp salt
- 1 tsp sugar
- 2 tbsp oil for sautéing
- 1 tsp lime juice (optional, for brightness)

Instructions:

Sprinkle the eggplant wedges lightly with salt and let them sit for about 10 minutes to draw out moisture. Pat them dry with paper towels. Heat oil in a frying pan over medium heat, and fry the eggplants until golden brown and tender. Set aside and drain any excess oil.

To make the balado sambal, blend the red chilies, bird's eye chilies, shallots, garlic, and tomatoes into a coarse paste. Heat 2 tablespoons of oil in a pan, then sauté the chili paste over medium heat until fragrant and the tomatoes are cooked down, about 5–7 minutes. Season with salt, sugar, and lime juice if using.

Add the fried eggplants to the sambal and toss gently until the eggplants are well coated. Let them simmer together for a few minutes so the flavors meld.

Serve Terong Balado warm or at room temperature with steamed rice — and enjoy the fiery, savory goodness of this beloved Indonesian dish.

Nasi Goreng

Prep Time
20 minutes

Cooking Time
15 minutes

Serving Size
4 servings

Ingredients:

- 4 cups cooked and cooled jasmine rice (preferably day-old)
- 200 g shrimp, peeled and deveined
- 200 g boneless chicken breast or thigh, diced
- 3 tbsp cooking oil
- 4 cloves garlic, minced
- 5 shallots, thinly sliced
- 2 red chilies, sliced (optional for spice)
- 2 tbsp sweet soy sauce (kecap manis)
- 1 tbsp soy sauce
- 1 tbsp oyster sauce
- 1/2 tsp ground white pepper
- Salt and sugar to taste
- 2 scallions, sliced

For Serving:

- Fried shallots
- 4 fried eggs, for serving
- Sliced cucumber and tomato
- Lime wedges
- Prawn crackers (kerupuk)

Instructions:

Heat 1 tablespoon of oil in a large wok or skillet over medium-high heat. Add the diced chicken and cook until lightly browned and cooked through, about 3–4 minutes. Add the shrimp and continue stir-frying until pink and opaque, then remove both from the pan and set aside.

Add the remaining oil to the pan. Sauté the garlic, shallots, and red chilies until fragrant and golden. Add the rice and break it up with the back of your spatula or spoon to avoid clumps. Return the cooked chicken and shrimp to the pan.

Pour in the sweet soy sauce, soy sauce, oyster sauce, white pepper, and a pinch of salt and sugar. Stir everything together thoroughly so the rice is evenly coated and heated through. Add the sliced scallions and stir for another minute.

Divide the fried rice among four plates and top each with a freshly fried egg—sunny side up is classic. Garnish with fried shallots, fresh vegetables, and prawn crackers if desired.

Enjoy this savory and satisfying Nasi Goreng with shrimp, chicken, and fried egg — a beloved Indonesian comfort dish!

Mie Goreng

Prep Time
15 minutes

Cooking Time
15 minutes

Serving Size
4 servings

Ingredients:

- 400 g dried egg noodles or instant noodles (without seasoning), cooked and drained
- 3 tbsp cooking oil
- 5 cloves garlic, minced
- 6 shallots, thinly sliced
- 2 eggs, beaten
- 2 tbsp sweet soy sauce (kecap manis)
- 1 tbsp regular soy sauce
- 1 tbsp oyster sauce
- 1 tsp sesame oil (optional)
- 1/2 tsp ground white pepper
- 1/2 tsp salt, or to taste
- 1/2 tsp sugar
- 200 g cabbage, thinly sliced
- 200 g pok choy or mustard green, sliced
- 2 scallions, sliced into 1-inch pieces

For Serving:
- Fried shallots
- 4 fried eggs, for serving
- Sliced cucumber and tomato
- Lime wedges

Instructions:

Heat the oil in a large wok or deep frying pan over medium heat. Sauté the garlic and shallots until fragrant and lightly golden. Pour beaten egg and stir-frying until just set. Add the sliced cabbage and pok choy, stir-frying for about 2–3 minutes until slightly softened. Toss in the cooked noodles, then pour in the sweet soy sauce, regular soy sauce, oyster sauce, sesame oil (if using), salt, sugar, and white pepper. Stir everything well to combine and coat the noodles evenly. Add the scallions, cooking for another 2–3 minutes. Taste and adjust seasoning if necessary.

Divide the noodles into four serving plates. Top each portion with a freshly fried egg, cooked to your liking—sunny side up is most traditional. Garnish with fried shallots and serve with cucumber slices, tomato wedges, and lime on the side for a fresh contrast.

Enjoy this comforting and flavorful Mie Goreng with fried egg as a satisfying meal any time of day!

Martabak Manis

Prep Time
1 hour

Cooking Time
20 minutes

Serving Size
4 servings

Ingredients:

Batter:
- 250 g all-purpose flour
- 50 g sugar
- 1/2 tsp salt
- 1/2 tsp baking soda
- 1/2 tsp baking powder
- 1 egg
- 300 ml water
- 1/2 tsp vanilla extract

After Resting (just before cooking):
- 1/2 tsp baking powder
- 1/2 tsp baking soda

Toppings (adjust to taste):
- 100 g sweetened condensed milk
- 100 g sugar
- 100 g grated cheddar cheese
- 100 g chocolate sprinkles
- 50 g crushed roasted peanuts
- Unsalted butter, for spreading

Instructions:

In a mixing bowl, combine flour, sugar, salt, baking soda, baking powder, egg, water, and vanilla extract. Whisk the ingredients until smooth and no lumps remain. Cover the batter and let it rest at room temperature for about 1 hour to allow it to develop flavor and air bubbles.

Once the batter has rested, stir in the additional baking powder and baking soda. Mix well just before cooking. Heat a non-stick pan with a heavy bottom or a martabak pan over medium-low heat. Lightly grease it with a little butter.

Pour in the batter to form a thick layer, about 1 to 2 cm thick. Spread it evenly and cook over low heat. When bubbles start to form and the surface looks set but still moist, cover the pan with a lid and let it steam for a few minutes until fully cooked. The bottom should be golden and the top fully set but still soft.

Remove the cooked martabak from the pan and immediately spread with generous amounts of butter while it's still hot. Sprinkle sugar, chocolate sprinkles, grated cheese, and crushed peanuts over the top, followed by drizzles of sweetened condensed milk.

Fold the martabak in half like a sandwich and press gently. Cut into portions and serve warm.

Enjoy this rich and indulgent Indonesian street snack, best eaten freshly made with melty toppings and a soft, spongy texture!

Es Cendol

Prep Time
30 minutes

Cooking Time
20 minutes

Serving Size
4 servings

Ingredients:

For the Cendol (Green Jelly):

- 100 g rice flour
- 30 g mung bean starch (or substitute with cornstarch)
- 500 ml pandan juice (blend pandan leaves with water, then strain)
- A pinch of salt
- Ice water (for setting the cendol)

For the Palm Sugar Syrup:

- 200 g palm sugar, chopped
- 100 ml water
- 1 pandan leaf, knotted

For the Coconut Milk:

- 400 ml coconut milk
- 1/4 tsp salt
- 1 pandan leaf, knotted

Additional Toppings:

- 150 g ripe jackfruit, thinly sliced
- Shaved ice or crushed ice

Instructions:

To make the cendol, mix rice flour, mung bean starch, pandan juice, and salt in a saucepan. Cook over medium heat while continuously stirring until the mixture thickens and turns into a smooth, sticky, and translucent green paste. Once thick, immediately transfer the paste into a cendol press or a colander with large holes, and press it over a bowl of ice water. Let the cendol strands set in the cold water until firm. Drain and set aside.

For the palm sugar syrup, combine chopped palm sugar, water, and pandan leaf in a saucepan. Heat over medium flame until the sugar melts completely and becomes syrupy. Strain to remove impurities and set aside to cool.

To prepare the coconut milk, simmer the coconut milk with salt and a pandan leaf over low heat. Stir constantly to prevent curdling. Once it begins to steam, turn off the heat and let it cool.

To assemble, divide the cendol evenly into 4 glasses. Add sliced jackfruit to each glass, followed by a generous spoonful of palm sugar syrup and chilled coconut milk. Top with plenty of shaved or crushed ice.

Enjoy this sweet, refreshing Es Cendol with Nangka, a perfect treat for hot days combining creamy coconut, fragrant pandan, rich palm sugar, and tropical jackfruit!

Printed in Dunstable, United Kingdom

7930l457R00045